# Make Money Blogging

*A Proven Method to*
*6 Figures A Year*

*By*

**Alain Magnuson**

This document is geared towards providing exact and reliable information in regards to the topic and issue covered. The publication is sold on the idea that the publisher is not required to render an accounting, officially permitted, or otherwise, qualified services. If advice is necessary, legal or professional, a practiced individual in the profession should be ordered.

- From a Declaration of Principles which was accepted and approved equally by a Committee of the American Bar Association and a Committee of Publishers and Associations.

The information provided herein is stated to be truthful and consistent, in that any liability, in terms of inattention or otherwise, by any usage or abuse of any policies, processes, or directions contained within is the

# DISCLAIMER

Any and all claims or representations as to income earnings are not to be considered as average earnings. Testimonials are not representative. There can by no assurances that any prior successes, or past results, as to income earnings, can be used as an indication of your future success or results.

Monetary and income results are based on many factors. The author has no way of knowing how well you will do, as he does not not know you, your background, your work ethic, or your business skills or practices. Therefore he can not guarantee or imply that you will win any incentives or prizes that may be offered, that you will make any income or earnings, that you will do well, or that you will make any money at all. If you rely upon our examples or figures, you do so at your own risk, and you accept all risk associated with your reliance.

Real property businesses and earnings derived therefrom, have unknown risks involved, and are not suitable for everyone. Making decisions based on any information presented in this book, should be done only with the

# Table of Contents

# INTRODUCTION

⌒

Blogging is still a wildly popular business model, and it has the power to help you earn six-figure incomes every single year. Many people dream of what life would be like if they could begin living remotely, blogging about the things that they love, and sharing their life with their followers while doing what they love. The reality is, this is actually not as hard as it may sound.

Many people believe that blogging is hard, or that it is too difficult to get yourself enough followers to actually make a profit. This is because most people don't realize that the process of building a profitable blog is more of a science than an art. There are specific strategies and elements to put in place that will help you maximize your profits, earn a healthy income, and live your desired life.

Blogging can provide you with both financial freedom and time freedom. This means that you can do virtually anything you desire with your life, while easily making money from anywhere you go. It is something that you can take with you, that can grow with you, and that can truly become a major part of your life. Most bloggers admit that the relationship they share with their fans and followers is one that they didn't expect and one that truly means a lot to them. You, too, can experience this if you begin building your blog properly!

"Make Money Blogging: A Proven Method for 6 Figures A Year" teaches you how to take blogging, apply the proven science for success, and begin earning financial and time freedom in your life. Each chapter will walk you through the guided step-by-step process to create the success you desire. This will ensure that you know exactly what you need to do to generate the success you crave, without any questions or confusion as to how to make it work.

How you choose to use this book is entirely up to you. However, it is recommended that you read it through once before you begin your blog. Doing this will ensure that you are clear on everything that needs to be done beforehand. Then, once you have a strong understanding of how each step leads to the next, you can return to the beginning. With your second read through, you can start applying the steps and generating massive success.

If you are ready to begin your blogging journey, as well as your journey to earning financial and time freedom, the time is now! Let's begin exploring how you can do all of this, easily, with zero confusion or questions. Take your time, have fun, and be sure to enjoy the process. Remember, freedom is what it is all about!

# CHAPTER I

~

# **Picking Your Topic**

Before you begin writing a blog, it is important that you choose your topic. You may or may not already have a topic in mind. If you do, I strongly encourage you to continue reading this chapter anyway. Reading this chapter will help you look deeper into the basis of your topic, determine whether or not it is actually profitable, and help you refine your topic so that you pick one that will take you to the top.

When you are choosing a blog topic to generate a six-figure income, you need to consider both your interests and the profitability of the topic. You are not simply writing for pleasure, but rather you are looking to turn your blog into a business. For that reason, you need to look at it from a business perspective.

## Brainstorm Topics You Enjoy

Before you begin looking into the profitability of topics, begin by brainstorming what types of things you enjoy talking about. Consider topics, but also consider niches. In general, most blogs perform best if you speak to a specific niche within an industry. So, try and consider what specific types of topics you like talking about, and which audiences you would enjoy interacting with the most.

It is important that you choose a topic that you genuinely enjoy. The idea of creating a blog that earns you six figures per year is typically built on the desire to have freedom. This should involve you considering both financial freedom, and time freedom. If you constantly feel annoyed or stressed about what you need to do for your blog, you are not going to experience time freedom. Furthermore, this will eventually lead to you not fully investing yourself in the business, and therefore you will not experience financial freedom, either.

Choosing a topic that you enjoy will assist you in feeling more confident in and excited by doing work for your blog. You will genuinely have fun when you get to research topics, write new content, and share it with your audience. This excitement will pour through in your writing and sharing, too. When people are passionate about what they write about, their audience can tell. This is usually what draws their audience in.

To make this step easy, start with at least three to five different topics that you would enjoy writing in most. That way, at least one of them should be a topic that you can easily profit from. If there is only one topic you really want to talk about, consider different angles or perspectives that you could approach it from to see if you can find unique niches around the topic. That way you can explore profitability and choose the option that is going to be the most fun to write and share about.

## Research These Topics

Once you have chosen which topics would excite you the most, you want to start to research these topics. How many blogs already exist in this niche? Are there any that are performing particularly well? What can you tell about these blogs? You want to collect as much information as you can about the topic itself. Notice how many blogs are already successful, and whether or not they are making a profit. Also, notice what angle they are taking on, and how popular the topic actually is.

The following three points in this chapter will point out the three things you need to consider most when you are researching a topic. By the time you research all three of these aspects, you should be left with one or two topics that are clearly superior to the others in regards to being worth the investment. If there is more than one, you get to decide which you would prefer to write in. Otherwise, stick to the one that is most likely to make you more money as this will be the best business decision.

## Consider Profitability

Profitability is a major key when you are looking to blog for, you know, profit. So, you need to consider the profitability of each niche. There are many ways that you can assess a topic for profitability. This will ensure that you can really consider how much profit you can actually make. After all, we are not looking for a couple hundred dollars here and there. We are looking to consistently make six-figure annual salaries through the blog. For that reason, we need a topic that is going to be highly profitable and successful.

The first thing that you want to do when you are checking for profitability is to bring up about ten blogs that each discuss the same topic you want to talk about. These should range in popularity from some of the biggest blogs in the niche to smaller and moderate-sized blogs. Then, you want to scan these blogs and see how profitable they actually are. Who is already making a profit on this topic? Are they making a decent profit? Where is their profit coming from, as far as you can tell? You can determine this by paying attention to monetized features. The most common sources on blogs include advertisements, sponsored posts, affiliate links, and products that are created by the bloggers themselves.

You want to get an idea of where the profits are coming from and how many avenues are being addressed in this way. That way, you can get a sense of just how profitable a blog topic can actually be. Remember, you don't want to pick one where you are only going to be able to make a limited income, you want to pick one where you will be able to make massive income. So, pay attention and look to see how many ways they are profiting.

Then, pay attention to the top bloggers. Your goal is to become amongst them, so you want to see the average income range for these bloggers. Since you have a goal of how much you want to make with your blog, you want to make sure that the top earners in your chosen industry are making about as much as you want to be making, if not more. If they aren't, there is a good chance that the topic you are looking into is not profitable enough for you to invest your time into it.

Once you have gone through all of the topics you chose and have determined their profitability, now you can begin to eliminate the ones that will not earn you a significant profit. After that, you can begin to move down the list of what you need to consider to ensure a topic is worthy of your attention!

## Consider Content Value

The next thing you need to focus on is content value. If you start a blog that is not going to give you plenty to talk about and with a great value attached, you are going to run dry quickly. You will not have the opportunity to make six figures from your blog because there simply won't be enough content to get you to that point. You have to make sure that the topic you are choosing to talk about is going to have plenty for you to discuss with your audience.

Go back to those ten blogs you selected to pay attention to and see what types of things they are talking about. Notice if these are topics that you would actually be interested in talking about and if they are going to be able to keep you sustained for a long time. Pay attention to see how many times they repeat similar topics, approach them from different angles, and recycle content. A blog may appear to have a lot to talk about, but upon closer inspection, you may realize that they actually do not have much new to talk about. This can result in you being run dry of topics and ultimately losing your audience. Alternatively, you may have to rebuild your audience consistently because your existing audience gets bored and moves on. If this is your goal, then choosing a topic like this is fine. If a six-figure income is your goal, then you need to choose a topic that will give you a lot to talk about.

After you have reviewed existing blogs, sit and brainstorm yourself. What topics do you think you would like to talk about? How many different topics can you come up with off the top of your head? Is it easy to draw on these ideas, or are you finding yourself struggling to come up with more? Knowing how easy it is to come up with fresh content will help you determine whether or not the topic can actually serve for a long time. Remember, you want to have plenty to talk about for a long time if you are going to grow your blog to a six-figure income earner.

Another thing you should consider is how well you know the content that you are considering writing about. While we can always research to freshen up or get more information on specific angles, writing about a topic that you know absolutely nothing about can prove to be difficult. While it does give you a chance to explore it, you will not connect well with your desired audience because they will end up clicking through to blogs that discuss the topic with greater certainty and knowingness. Choose a topic that is easy for you to talk about and that you have a strong basic understanding of at the very least. This will ensure that when you talk about the topic, you can speak with authority, and people are more likely to listen to you. If you speak too timidly or regularly recite wrong facts or information that does not make sense, people will begin to realize that you are not a reliable source and they will go elsewhere for their information.

## Consider Your Audience

Finally, you must consider your audience! There are a few ways that you can factor in your audience. Since you don't actually have one already, you need to consider who your audience is going to be.

One great way is to take a look at your existing audience. Although it may not be much beyond your friends and family, consider the ones that you speak with most about this specific subject on. What is it about them that keeps you talking about this subject? How do they resemble the audience that you may eventually speak to openly on your blog? Pay attention to these factors and use them to begin generating an ideal audience.

Another thing you should consider is who the audience of your competition's blogs are. Pay attention to blogs that are similar to what yours will be and consider who they are speaking to. This will be very similar to the audience you want to speak to, so paying attention to this information and generating an understanding of who their audience is can help you when it comes to knowing who you are talking to.

Finally, consider who you want to talk to. What audience excites you the most? What is it about them that makes you eager to talk to them and share your information with them? Why are they the best people for you to speak to? How can you serve them? Get clear on the specifics between you and them. You want to consider your audience because this is how you are going to pick your final topic. Your final topic should align with an audience that you feel comfortable speaking to from a place of authority. If you don't, you are going to struggle to position yourself as an expert and acquire readers and people who are willing to listen to you.

## The Final Pick

The topic you end up picking should be one that will provide you with ample opportunity to generate your desired income, that will have plenty for you to talk about, and that will speak directly to your desired audience. You should know how to approach your audience, communicate with your audience, and keep your audience. If you want to generate six-figure earnings with your blog, you do not want to choose an audience that will come and go quickly. Instead, you want to build a relationship with your audience and keep them coming back for a long time. This will ensure that you can build your audiences loyalty and, later, capitalize on that loyalty!

# CHAPTER 2

❧

# **Choose Your Design**

Now that you know what you want to talk about and who you want to be talking to, you need to begin thinking about what you want your blog to look like. Believe it or not, the design of your blog plays a big role in how people will perceive you. Experts say that if a person lands on your website and is not clear on what to do or attracted to it within the first 10 seconds, they will just as quickly click back off of your website. This means that you have to capture their attention and drive their focus in about 10 seconds. Your design is exactly what will help you with that.

When it comes to a blog, you do not need to invest in a fancy or expensive web designer to get it to where you want to be. At least, not right away. If that is something you choose to invest in later in the future, that is a great idea. This can help maximize the flow of your website, increase the aesthetics, and take you from small-time professional to the big leagues. Still, it is not necessary early on. In fact, it is not even recommended early on. While you do want an appealing and easy-to-navigate website, you do not want to go into debt before you start earning income. Wait until your blog begins generating a steady income before you begin investing in expensive designers and graphics. In the meantime, take advantage of these four tips to help you.

**Think About What You Like**

You have already been browsing other blogs to get an idea of what topic is going to help you generate success. So, that means you have already been navigating other blogs that are similar to the one that you want to create. By now, you should have a pretty clear understanding in regards to what you like and what you don't like on a blog. You may have encountered various features or graphics that drew you in and others that you were not attracted to at all. Consider these reactions. These will help you determine how you want your own blog to look.

Although your blog appearance is meant to draw others in, remember that you should enjoy it, too. If you do not enjoy the blog that you are creating, you simply won't feel the drive to continue working toward it. Getting to that point will take a significant amount of time and energy, and it won't feel good creating financial freedom for yourself. You should enjoy this process as much as your audience will.

## Choose One That Will Reflect Your Topic

Another thing that you need to consider that many people don't is how your design reflects your topic. Believe it or not, different aesthetics are used depending on what you are talking about. If you are talking about a topic that involves a lot of pictures, such as photography, you will want a design that highlights the photographs you are taking while also providing ample space for you to share your verbal opinion. If your topic revolves more about opinion and topics, however, and not graphics, you may want one that highlights your conversation more.

Additionally, the entire format of your page varies depending on who you are targeting. Some blogs will revolve solely around blog entries, whereas others feature other pages, too. These sometimes include "evergreen content," such as your most popular blog posts or ones that tend to be read more than once, resources, product information, and guides, or even various categories of your blog itself. Pay attention to what you want your design to feature so that you can choose one that is going to allow you to accurately reflect the topic that you are talking about.

## Pick One That Is Aesthetically Appealing

Remember, the first ten seconds are all you have to draw someone in. You need to pick a blog that is going to be aesthetically appealing, and that will draw people in right away. They should feel immediately drawn in to look further. Consider your design your packaging. This is the "packaging" that your blog is packed in, and if it is not appealing, people likely won't care about what is inside. Instead, they will be drawn to look elsewhere.

It may sound shallow, but aesthetics amount to a lot when it comes to blogging. You need a design that has easy to read colors, graphics that are attractive and focused, and a clear "purpose." People should land on your blog and know exactly what topic you will be discussing in all of your content. There should be no guessing or confusion. They should also immediately be drawn to the key areas of your blog. For example, your blog itself, or your products or services associated with your blog.

Finally, you need an aesthetic and design that works. There is nothing worse than landing on a blog where the design does not flow well, pages are not properly designed, and ultimately you are uncertain about how anything works. Broken hyperlinks, incomplete pages, an enormous number of visible grammatical and spelling errors, and other such factors can quickly drive people to search for the same content elsewhere. Your page design should function properly if you are going to get anything from it. Think about professionalism in every way that you can, especially with your design.

## Consider What Your Audience Would Like

Remember, your blog is not just about you. You need to consider what your audience is going to be most drawn to, too. This is a great opportunity for you to go back to those ten blogs you originally researched and look them over once more. What do the most popular blogs have in common? What do the least popular blogs in common? Can you say anything apart based on how they are designed? Often, the more popular blogs will have common features and so, too, will the least popular ones. Pay attention to these themes and trends, as you will want to implement the ones being used by the popular blogs. This is how you can make your blog look "flashy" and professional right from the start. Learn from the mistakes of other bloggers in regards to their design so that when it comes to your own blog, you can skip past the mistakes and errors and move straight toward success!

## Your Host

The last element you need to consider when you are discussing your design is the host that you are going to use. There are many popular hosts out there. If you are already using a host, you may simply want to stay with them for now. Otherwise, you may want to switch to one of the more popular ones. Currently, the most popular blog hosts right now are:

- Squarespace
- WordPress (.com not .org if you are a beginner. Only use .org if you have experience with coding, or have access to someone who does.)
- HostGator
- BlueHost

Bloggers everywhere, even the more successful ones, claim that these are the best ones to invest in. They are easy for beginners to use, but also provide you with ample professionalism so that you can design a blog that looks amazing. Choosing your host is vital, as switching hosts can prove to be rather difficult once your blog is established. Pick one that you are going to be able to use for a long time. While you can certainly switch in the future, the idea is to prolong that need for as long as possible, or potentially never face it, to begin with!

Once you have chosen your host, go ahead and integrate your design and build the basics of your blog. Begin with a basic design, then go in and perfect everything to your preferences. Make it look your best, but do not get overly hung up on perfectionism here. Although the aesthetic element is important, most people are looking for an attractive aesthetic, not a perfect one. Several blogs are generating wonderful success despite not having completely perfect designs. The main idea is to keep it attractive and functional.

# CHAPTER 3

~

# **Create Your Articles**

With your topic outlined and your design nailed down, it is time to create your articles. Your articles are what people are going to be looking for, interacting with, talking about, sharing, and ultimately coming back for. For that reason, this would be the area where you really want to let your perfectionism fly! While you don't have to be overly perfect, this is where you want to put your best quality work into. If you are not proud of it, do not release it. Releasing content that you are not proud of or that does not meet your specific topic or aesthetic will quickly result in you losing followers, or not gaining any traction, to begin with.

Every time you create content, consider how it compares to your design and your topic. You want to build a brand through this all, so you need to make sure that all three of these elements align effectively. Speak on-brand, keep your graphics and aesthetics on-brand, and remain as consistent as possible across all of this. This will ensure that you are staying consistent and clear to your audience and that they know exactly what to expect when they come to your page or read your content.

In addition to remaining consistent, the following six tools will help ensure that you are creating catchy, valuable, and likable content that your audience will love. Put these tools into effect, and you will be sure to generate content that people will be eager to read about and share with others. This will help you grow your audience, as well as grow audience loyalty!

## Set a Schedule

Blogs that do not have a consistent schedule can become difficult for people to follow and remain loyal to. This means that people will know exactly when they can expect new content to come out and they can look for it when it does. They know that you are reliable, they look forward to your content and then check in on the days when you are going to be releasing content.

Setting a schedule does not mean that you cannot begin adding more information to your blog on top of your existing schedule. It simply means that your audience will know exactly what to expect and when. It also means that you know when you need to have content done by. If you find that you are an inconsistent writer and that sitting down a few times a week to write new content is not easy for you, consider writing as much as you can on an ongoing basis and scheduling posts ahead of time so that they are already prepared to be released. Alternatively, you can keep some "back up posts" written that you keep on hand and use if you find that your scheduled post is due to be released and you have yet to write anything. Writer's block is a very real thing, and preparing for it and having content prepared in advance can ensure that you are not releasing content strictly because of your schedule and that everything you release continues to be high quality.

## Brainstorm Content

Many bloggers believe that regularly brainstorming content is a great way to make sure that you are coming up with the best stuff. Keeping a pen and notebook nearby is a great way to ensure that you are always ready to jot down any ideas that come to mind. Brainstorm as often as ideas come to you. Before you actually begin writing, unless you know exactly what you want to talk about, brainstorm more! Brainstorming like this does not mean that you are going to write about every single topic you come up with. However, it does help you sort through everything that you are thinking about and find the topics that are going to add the most value to your blog and be the best received by your audience.

Once you have effectively brainstormed, you can then go back to the many ideas that you came up with and choose the best one. Chances are you've come up with several great ones. This means you will have plenty to talk about for your next several posts! Simply pick the one that is most relevant to what is going on lately, or that you are most excited to talk about and begin writing on that topic!

## Stay On-Topic

You absolutely must stay on-topic. This works in two ways: you need to stay on-topic with your blog topic itself, and you need to stay on-topic with the post topic. If your blog promises to talk about travel, everything you talk about should somehow be related to travel. If your post promises to talk specifically about the best places to stay in Bali, then you should only be talking about this topic itself. Going off-topic with your blog itself, or with posts, can confuse your audience. They will end up wondering what you are talking about, finding themselves confused about why this is relevant to what they clicked in to learn about and may result in them feeling like your blog is spam.

These days, there is a strategy that many bloggers use known as "click-bait." This is where they choose a title that says one thing, but the entire article is about something else. The article typically does not provide value, nor does it actively discuss the promised topic nearly as much as they make you believe it will. Blogs do this because it gets more people visiting their page, which drives it up higher in the search engines (SEO). This means they get more hits and therefore can increase their own monetized values because they can claim that they get several unique blog visitors. It may work in the short-term, but in the long run, it completely tarnishes the blog's reputation. It is not ideal. If you want to avoid being viewed as an individual who makes use of click-bait, make sure that all of your posts are on-topic and that they stay to the point that you promised to talk about in your title.

## Use Popular Templates or Writing Styles

There are certain styles of blogs that seem to perform better than other styles. These are considered templates because they have the same structure and you simply change the content that you place within the body of the blog itself. This may sound as though it will not serve in the long run, but the reality is that it actually will. Many of these templates are already known to perform incredible results because they provide content in ways that the person's audience genuinely enjoys receiving content.

These templates include:

- Lists. Lists come in two formats. One is a small bite-sized list with three to five tips you can "quickly implement" right away to get a certain set of results. The other type of list is one that is exhaustive and contains upward of 10 items that will give you "all of the information on" any particular topic in an easy-to-understand format.

- Parody. Lately, parody blog posts have grown in popularity. People love hopping onto these posts and seeing people poking fun at stereotypes and playing around with sarcasm. They help break up the seriousness in a tone that many other blog posts may have.

- Trending. Talking about things that are trending and incorporating your own style or flair into the topic is another great way. These are typically

1000 words or less in length and have some form of a unique angle on the latest trends in your industry. Sometimes, they may also take global trends and uniquely shape them to work for their industry, even if they are not industry-specific or even traditional to the industry of the blog itself.

These three formats seem to produce the best results in regards to getting people to your website and providing them with content that they are willing to read. While longer posts and other formats can certainly generate a buzz in your long-term visitors, these formats seem to be the best for those who are unfamiliar with who you are or what you are talking about. Even with loyal viewers, these types of posts give them quick access to bite-sized pieces of information that they can consume in five minutes or less. This gives them all that they want to know in a quick, clean, unique, and quirky manner that is unique to your personality. This is what audiences love!

## Come Up with Catchy Titles

Your title is the first thing people are going to see before they begin reading your post. For that reason, you need to pick one that is catchy and interesting. If your title is highly focused and clear on the topic you will be talking about but does not come across as interesting, people are going to be far less likely to read anything that you have written. It is important that you come up with catchy titles.

There are a few tips and tricks that you can take into consideration when it comes to creating titles for your posts. While they should always be focused on the content of the article itself, they should also be catchy. So, stay honest but have fun with it! Some tips you can take advantage of include:

- Creating a title that promises to give more information about a fascinating but reveals nothing. Using "…" at the end is a great way to build suspense and interest.

- Use alliteration. "Suzy's Super Summer Savings List," for example. People love reading catchy titles like this, it rolls well off of the tongue and feels fun to say. As a result, they are more likely to be interested in what the article itself is all about.

- Be cheesy. Seriously, people love cheesy topics. For example, use dry jokes or puns in your title. "Get A Load of This New Laundry Soap!" would be great if you were a lifestyle blog that discusses safe and natural cleaning alternatives. Or, "Why Did the Chicken Cross the Street? To Grab a Pair of These!" if you are a fashion blog that is talking about a new pair of shoes or pants that you want people to check out. Using corny jokes like this is a great way to get people smiling and gain their interest in what you are talking about.

The ultimate way to come up with great titles is to really think about what is going to make people smile or wonder "what?" You want people to know the answer or become curious about what is within the body of your post. That way, they are going to be more likely to click on the title and begin exploring what you are talking about. If they like it, they will also click through and explore more of your posts! As a result, you may just end up with a new loyal reader.

## Consider Your Graphics

Graphics on a blog are vital. Even though the primary point of a blog typically revolves around the content and written materials, the graphics are important, too. Providing graphics within your post gives your readers a great opportunity to feel "rewarded" for reading. It is said that providing at least one image per 1000 words written is a great way to break up all of the words. When your article is visibly appealing based on how it is designed, the font that is used, and the graphics involved, people are far more likely to stick around and read it.

Remember, the aesthetics are what draw people in. You have about 10 seconds to win them over and keep their attention. If your blog graphics and aesthetics on each post are not fulfilling enough, people will likely click away. Graphics give you the opportunity to add an attractive element to your blog posts and keep people on them long enough to actually read what you have to say.

## Putting It All Together

Early on, writing your content may seem a little intimidating. There are many aspects to consider when you are writing content for a blog. The best thing you can do is put it in order, work one at a time, and then put it all together. When you get used to writing, as well as the receptiveness of your unique audience, it will become a lot easier to learn about what they are actually interested in and how you can write specifically for them. As a result, you will find creating content much easier. The best thing you can do in the beginning is to experiment and then pay attention to your analytics, which you will learn more about in Chapter 5: "Monitor Your Analytics."

To recap, here is a checklist for you to consider when you are creating new content for your blog:

- Brainstorm a topic, pick one that serves your audience right now
- Ensure that your topic is on-brand for your blog
- Create content that is relevant to your chosen topic
- Write in a popular style format that will appeal to your audience
- Create a catchy title that will draw people in
- Add graphics that will keep people on your page after the 10-second check

As long as you meet all of these criteria, you are sure to create incredible content that your audience will love. Again, if you are brand new, don't worry if it is not entirely well received in the beginning. First off, many people are still just learning about you. Second, you are still learning about your audience and what they like most. Use this as an opportunity to find where your unique spot is inside of your niche, and then leverage this to help you create even better content each time.

# CHAPTER 4

❧

# Focus on Growing Your Audience

Something that you have to recognize in the blogging world is that, no matter how great your content is, you are not going to get any readers if you don't focus on growing your audience! Fortunately, growing your audience does not require you to invest significant amounts of money into advertisements and promotion. While this is certainly an option, and we will discuss it, the reality is that the best ways to promote your blog are actually free. You should only begin seeking to implement paid advertisements after you have a steady audience and are getting regular visitors to your page.

## Look Beyond Your Website

Until now, a large portion of your focus has been built solely on your website. You have focused on your topic, your design, and your content. Now, you need to begin looking outside of your website. You have done all that you can on your website to align yourself with your target audience and draw them in, but now you need to focus on creating "funnels" to draw them in through.

Funnels are a business term used to describe all of the efforts we put in to various areas of draw people in to what we ultimately want them to land on. As a blogger, all of your external efforts are primarily focused on drawing people in to your blog itself. So, everything you do should ultimately be focused on drawing people in toward reading the posts you are posting and exploring the rest of the content that resides on your website.

You can do this through social media, paid advertisements, word of mouth, collaborations, contests, and even through business cards, flyers, and other in-person platforms that allow you to connect with your audience. Ultimately, anything that can help you drive traffic back toward your blog is a positive practice.

However, there are some things you need to consider. Primarily, you want to be focusing your efforts entirely on those that are returning great results. If you are putting effort into bringing people in and a certain method is not returning positive results, or the results are not worth the amount of investment it takes to get those results, then you likely want to cut that effort out. Instead, you can move toward focusing your energy on areas where the return on your time and financial investments are high.

## Build an Online Presence

The biggest way to drive traffic to your blog is through having an online presence. Building your blog as a brand and then showing up online in various areas is a great way to make sure that you are interacting with your audience. This is how you can get in front of them on a regular basis, engage with your audience, connect with them more personally than a strictly blog-based presence allows for, and ultimately put your content in front of these people in the end. As you know, the entire purpose is to drive them back to your website.

Which social media websites you focus on will largely depend on who your target audience consists of. Facebook is generally a great place to start as nearly every audience exists on Facebook. However, determining whether Twitter, Instagram, YouTube, or other channels are going to be worthwhile or not will depend on where your audience hangs out the most. You can usually figure this out quickly through an internet search. I would provide you with a list, but the places where people hang out online is regularly changing and, therefore, it would be hard for that list to remain consistent or accurate for long. Instead, it is best if you take a look and pay attention to the current stats based on when you are starting your blog, or when you are looking to take it to the next level.

When you are building an online presence, treat your social media as both a separate entity from your blog and a driving force for your blog. So, not every post should be specifically about your blog posts and topics you have talked about on your blog. Instead, post-organic content loaded with great information, interesting topics, humor, and attractive or funny pictures that will get your audience paying attention. The more that you interact with them, the better this will be for your traffic.

Your online presence will rely on three things: consistency, targeted content, and engagement. You should be posting at least three times a week, though daily is typically better. This keeps you relevant, at the top of the newsfeed, and regularly being exposed to the opportunity for people to see you and engage with your content. Then, you need to make sure that the content you are posting is actually stuff that people want to engage with. It should be interesting or attractive in some form so that it allows for people to truly want to get involved and start communicating with you, or at least liking and/or sharing your content. Then, when people do communicate with you through your social media platforms, be sure to comment back! Chat with them, show that you see them, and ultimately create a back-and-forth form of engagement so that your audience knows that you appreciate them and their loyalty. People who engage back with their audience are known to get far more loyalty and engagement to begin with, so this is definitely something you need to pay attention to. Regular engagement in this way will mean that every time you post a new blog post, you are more likely to drive people to your site through your social media as a result of the loyalty you have established.

## Seek to Network with Others

When it comes to blogging, you do not have to be in a dog-eat-dog world. What that means is, you are not required to "hold your own" and stay completely in competition with other blogs in your niche. In fact, networking can be one of the most powerful moves that you make. When you put your name out there and get into the eyes of other bloggers, you open up a major potential for you to be further shared around. Because you begin to develop a relationship with these bloggers, they are more likely to refer people to your content when they see stuff that you've posted that they feel their audience will resonate with. The same should go in reverse, too. When they send people your way and support your growth, do the same for them! Network, and expand your audience.

In addition to simply chatting about each other's presence, networking allows you to open up the opportunity for collaborations. Collaborations in the blogging world mean posts that are done by two or more bloggers to provide even greater value for each of your unique audiences. If collaborations don't make sense or work for you, you can also use guest posting features as an opportunity for you to expand your network, and your reach. Opening up your blog for guest posters, or featuring on someone else's blog means that you both get the opportunity to cross-promote to each other's audiences. This means that you expand your reach and more people will begin to know who you are.

Networking in the blogging field is actually an incredible asset to have. Bloggers tend to band together to form a sort of community, and this community leads to each person within the community growing more successfully as a result of the shared support and promotion. By building a community of your own within the blogging industry with the help of other bloggers, you allow this form of cross-promotion and collective growth to take place. Naturally, this means great things for your own blog.

## Consider Paid Promotions

While they are absolutely not necessary and are not ideal for someone with zero audiences, paid promotions can hold great value for those who already have a basic audience-generated. When you know who your audience is, your growth through promotions is a lot easier to create.

The key to paid promotions is that you have to know who you are targeting in your advertisements. If you have not yet found your "spot" in the blogging world, then you have yet to actually discover exactly who your audience consists of. The reality is that in most cases, which we think our audience will be who they actually are can vary. For that reason, you do not want to be wasting any of your valuable income on ads that are unlikely to effectively reach your target audience and gain you any form of return. Instead, you want to wait until you have an audience that is already creating some form of engagement and giving you feedback.

Once you have developed a clear basis for this analytics, however, you can begin using paid advertisements as an opportunity to promote your blog. In the beginning, start smaller until you begin to understand which advertisements work the best. Then, you can start investing more into paid advertising. When done properly and implemented at the right times, paid advertising can certainly be a valuable asset to growth. In fact, many people swear by it. The great thing about paid advertising is that one single advertisement can reach many, many people outside of your existing audience. This somewhat automates your growth and increases your growth ratios exponentially, if done properly.

Still, I can't stress enough that you should not invest in paid promotions until you have a fairly consistent audience in place. Once you do, begin looking at Google AdWords and various social media advertising platforms to provide you with the best opportunity to reach your audience. Ideally, you want to promote on the same social media platforms where you already get your highest levels of engagement. This is because this clearly proves that this is where a large amount of your audience hangs out and that you are more likely to get a great return here.

# CHAPTER 5

⌐

# Monitor Your Analytics

Since you are running your blog with the intention of making funds from it, you need to regard it as a business. As with any business, your analytics play a huge role in helping guide you through the process of growing your blog and maximizing your income and profitability. By paying attention to this important analytics, you give yourself the opportunity to discover where your biggest growth resides, how you can amplify that growth, and what strategies you need to enforce further to create the results that you desire. In this chapter, we are going to explore what your analytics are, how you can pay attention to them, and what they tell you in terms of where your growth potential lies.

## What Are Analytics?

Analytics is like your "results." These are the statistics that show you how successfully (or not) a certain effort performed. Blog posts, social media posts, advertisements, and other outreach efforts are all gauged based on how well they have performed. By paying attention to these results, you can analyze the success of various strategies, and thus, you can locate where the maximum opportunity for success resides.

Your analytics are typically posted for you in the backend of your blog hosting platform, on the backend of your social media managers, and in other locations. Paying attention to these results can significantly boost your ability to know what you should do to maximize growth.

Logically, you want to do more of what gets you better engagement and results, and less of what doesn't. So, when you are paying attention to analytics, you want to be paying attention to both sides of the spectrum. Look at what people were most interested in, and what they were least interested in. Then, when you have, you can also pay attention to how these posts and outreach strategies differed, and what that means for you. Ultimately, you want to take these as "lessons" that you can use to guide you through future outreach efforts.

## Pay Attention to Popular Titles and Articles

The first thing you want to pay attention to when you are looking into your analytics is what was the most popular. You want to see what people clicked onto most, which titles earned the highest number of likes and shares, and where people were getting the most engaged. Paying attention to these posts is going to give you ample information on what people are interested in, what they want to see more of, and how you can tailor future content to serve your audience.

Since this is where the majority of your information will come from, some believe that you should go beyond going into each individual metric system attached to each account to monitor your analytics. I would have to agree.

The best way to do this is to open some form of document on your computer and begin posting the links to the content that performed the best, as well as specific metrics. For example, how many hits the page got, how many likes or shares it got, how many people commented, and what platform it was posted on. You can also include information about how you promoted this content if you did. You should also jot down some form of notes outlining primary points associated with each post so that you can begin to recognize themes and trends in your popular titles and posts. This puts everything in one place so that it is easy to see where your success lies.

## Collect Data to See What Exactly People Like

Like we discussed above, the idea is to get a very clear idea of what people like. As you are collecting your data, putting together trends and themes and following those is a great way to make sure that you are staying on top of everything and that you are learning the most that you can about what your followers like. This gives you the opportunity to see what it is that draws them in, to begin with.

When you know what draws people in, it becomes a lot easier to incorporate more of that in future content. This means that you can begin specifically tailoring your content, both through blog posts and outreach efforts such as on social media, for your audience. Through these efforts, it becomes a lot easier to post more of what your audience is likely to share and like. The more they engage, the better your outreach will perform. Then, as a result, your audience will begin to rapidly grow.

## Be Sure to Consider What People Don't Like, Too

When you are collecting analytics, it is always important to consider both ends of the spectrum, too. This would be anywhere where posts don't perform well. Now, before you begin inspecting underperforming posts, it is important to know what an underperforming post actually looks like.

As you begin to post more content, you will likely notice that you have an average. For example, maybe your average engagement is something like 1000 viewers per post. So, a post that is performing exceptionally would be any post with more than, say, 1100 viewers, with more being even better. A post that would be underperforming, however, would be one with significantly fewer viewers than 1000. Say, 900 or less. When you find a post that has significantly fewer views than your average, it is important that you analyze this post, too.

When you analyze these underperforming posts, the goal is to understand why they performed poorly. What did you do differently with this post that resulted in it not performing as well? You want to identify what it was that resulted in people not being as drawn into it or as interested in it. This will help you ensure that you don't carry these ineffective strategies forward and potentially damage your growth by doing things your audience doesn't respond well to.

Understanding both ends of the spectrum allows you to do more of what your audience does like, and less of what they don't like, every single time. This is how you can maximize your viewership by making sure that you are paying close attention to what your audience wants and needs.

## Post More Content That Will Earn Likes and Shares

Now that you have a clear understanding of what you are looking for in regards to what your audience likes and dislikes, it's time to start creating more content that they are going to respond well to! Consider your analytics direct feedback toward what your audience wants you to talk about and share. Then, with that knowledge, you simply agree! Talk about the topics they enjoy, use titles that they respond well to, post in areas that they tend to spend time in, post at the right time of day, and follow all of the trends that you have discovered in your analysis. By following these strategies, you can ensure that you are going to have major success in the long run.

## Never Stop Checking Your Analytics

Before we end the discussion on analytics, we need to get clear on one very important thing. There is never a time in your blogging career where you should stop performing analytic checks. Every week or every month, whichever works best for you, you need to be checking analytics. This is how you can ensure that you are staying on top of trends and themes. As you likely already know, trends and themes change rapidly. Staying on top of your analytics allows you to be ahead of the curve.

If you ever stop checking on your analytics, you can almost certainly guarantee that your success is going to begin to fall. This is because you are no longer listening to your audience and producing content that directly relates to what they have "asked" for. As a result, they are no longer tuning in to what you are saying.

If you are only blogging for fun, then you can stop checking analytics and follow whatever trend it is that you want to. However, if you want to blog to earn an annual salary of six figures per year, you need to stay focused on your analytics. These act as a form of compass to guide you in the proper direction, and ignoring them may result in you losing out on major success, and therefore major profitability!

# CHAPTER 6

∽

# Monetize Through Ads

Now that you are aware of how you can start, develop, and grow your blog, it is time to get into the good stuff. That is, monetization! In the following chapters, we are going to explore how you can monetize your blogs. We are going to focus on the three largest sources of income for all bloggers and how you can begin tapping into these sources. You will also learn about when you can begin using these forms of monetization to make sure that you deploy them at the right time so that you can maximize profits.

The first area we are going to focus on is advertisements. Advertisements are a major source of income for bloggers, and they provide you with ample opportunity to create this income early on.

## When to Sell Ad Space

Knowing when to sell ad space is important. As with anything, pulling the trigger at the right time can have a major impact when it comes to how well it serves you. The greatest part of advertisements is that, for the most part, you can begin selling ad space on your blog right away. This answer may seem straightforward, and in reality, it is. However, certain circumstances may force you to hold off before you can start.

The biggest thing that prevents people from selling ad space right away is host policies. Some platforms have policies about when you can begin selling ad space on your blog. This is an effort to reduce spam pages. For hosts, having authentic pages that add value means that they are regarded with greater respect. Therefore, they are often very careful to ensure that none of the pages they are hosting come off as spam. For that reason, you may find that certain hosts have policies that prevent you from selling ad space early on.

Another thing you need to be aware of is that some hosts do not integrate with certain popular advertisement companies at all. For example, not all hosts support Google Ads. Therefore, if you use a host that does not support these ads, you cannot use Google Ads as a source of income on your blog. These are things you need to consider beforehand, to ensure that you can begin monetizing as soon as possible.

## How to Properly Sell Ad Space On Your Blog

Now that you understand when you can start selling ad space on your blog, you are likely curious to know how you can do so properly. First, you need to make sure that you comply with the policies of both your platform host and the company that you are advertising for. Everything on your website should be in compliance to ensure that you don't run into any issues later on. If you are not compliant, this could warrant your profits worthless and result in them being taken away due to your lack of compliance. Since this is your business and your income we are talking about, it is important that you take these things seriously and that you protect your profitability.

Next, you need to know how much advertisement space is actually appropriate to sell. Many websites out there have far too many advertisements on their page. While they may earn them some income, it will also significantly decrease their number of loyal followers. The reality is, blog readers do not want to have advertisements blasted at them, popping up, and taking over most of the screen. First, they are not aesthetically appealing for the most part. When there are too many, they clash and become overwhelming. Second, they take away from the reading experience. People are so busy scrolling through ads to get to your content that it becomes more hassle than it's worth and they stop doing it. Third, ads can take an enormous amount of time to load. One or two is typically easy for an average device to quickly load, but when you get too many, it takes forever for the page to actively load. This means most people will close the site because you don't pass the 10-second rule.

When you are selling ad space, you need to ensure that you are not overwhelming your website with advertisements. Having one or two per page is a great way to ensure that you can bring in an income through advertisements, but that you are not overwhelming your audience. You should also refrain from having any on your homepage, as this is tacky. This means that they will be far more likely to maintain their loyalty and continue coming back. People typically appreciate when a blog hosts advertisements because they recognize this as an opportunity to sustain the blog. However, once they start seeing too many advertisements, they begin to feel like the only purpose of the blog is to generate money and not create valuable content. As a result, how they perceive your entire brand and image will be deteriorated. Being mindful of the amount of ad space you are selling on your page will ensure that you maintain your loyal following and that you can begin generating a sustainable income.

## Advertisement Companies and Agencies

The first way that you can begin selling ad space tends to be the easiest way, too. This involves you getting started with a company, such as Google Ads. You create a profile, proof your website, and then get approved for your contract. Then, you can choose how many ads you want to display on your website, and where. Google will then target your readers with advertisements based on their unique algorithms. All you really have to do is plug in your profile, place the coding on your website, and let Google do the rest. As a result, you get paid for the ad space.

Google is not the only company that has this style of advertisement selling. There are many other agencies that you can go through, too. Another popular alternative includes Amazon. Choosing these larger companies tends to make the process significantly easier. This is because they specialize in advertisements. Therefore, they make the process incredibly easy for you. To them, the easier it is for you to get started, the more likely you will choose them. Then, as a result, they have more ad space to sell and can make more money from their clients. You, in turn, make more money as well.

## Private Selling of Ad Space

The other strategy you can use to sell ad space is private selling. This essentially means that you offer to create an advertisement block for a company and feature it on your page. This company then directly pays you for the space on your website. Doing this can make it slightly harder to get deals, especially if you are new. However, the larger your blog gets, the more money you stand to make doing this. Still, it does take a lot of work and time. You need to ensure that you set the contracts, that you collect payments, that the advertisements are attractive and high quality, and that you stay on top of relevancy. You don't want to be hosting an ad longer than someone has paid for, so you need to be very aware of timelines. You also need to constantly be selling this space, which can result in you investing money directly into this purpose.

While the private selling of ad space does allow for you to choose your price and potentially make more money, it does also require an investment itself. Both time and financial investments are required for you to make any form of income with selling private ad space. If you have the time and resources, this can be a great way to maximize your ad space profits. Otherwise, it may be best to stick to agencies.

## Types of Advertisements

There are many different types of advertisements that exist that can be displayed on websites. However, the two most common ones include banner advertisements and block advertisements. Banners are typically long, short picture-style advertisements that are displayed in the header or footer of a website. They are great for catching attention. They also tend to earn more money because they take up more space and have a tendency to perform better than other advertisements.

Block advertisements are typically square, or slightly rectangular but more like a picture than a long rectangular banner. These range in size, taking up as little as a couple of inches in the corner of the screen, to several inches on an entire page. The larger the ad, the more you typically make due to it taking up more space on your website. These are popular when they are scattered into posts themselves, and placed strategically around the website.

Ideally, you want to use both forms of advertisements on your website. One or two block advertisements and a banner advertisement is a fairly good ratio. If possible, only have the banners on certain pages. Having them all on every page can become a little overwhelming since they tend to take up a lot of space.

## How You Get Paid

Getting paid for ad space works in one of two ways: either you are paid for the placement of the ad itself, or you are paid every time the ad is clicked on. The latter is known as "Pay-Per-Click" or "PPC" for short.

Evergreen payments are less common in the advertisement industry in terms of agencies, as this tends to cost them more money than they stand to make. Overall, it would be a poor business move for the agency. However, this is a popular payment format for privately selling ad space. This is also why you stand to make significantly more in privately selling your ad space on your website. When you sell privately, you typically want to collect payment before the ad is ever posted on your website. How you collect your payment will depend on your preferences.

PPC is the more common payment method used by advertisement agencies, as you are essentially getting paid a commission to drive traffic to their website. If you have an active and engaged audience that regularly clicks to your website, this can be a great way to maximize your income while automating the process. The agencies automatically target your audience based on their unique cookies and browsing patterns so each person will see an advertisement for something different on the page. This means that they are far more likely to click through and earn you some income. When you collect payment from an agency, it will typically be paid out once or twice per month either to your PayPal account or directly to your bank account. Sometimes, it may simply be issued to your account itself, and it is up to you to choose how you want to withdraw it so that you can access your funds. You should also note that some agencies have a minimum payout amount, so if you don't meet that amount, you may not be able to access your funds until you do. This shouldn't matter, however, once your blog gets bigger as you should be regularly going far over the minimum payout amount!

CHAPTER 7

# Monetize Through Sponsored Content

The next popular way to monetize your blog is through sponsored content. This becomes more popular as your blog grows, as sponsors are typically looking for an active, proven, and loyal following in their bloggers. Once you have developed a consistent audience that is rapidly growing, you can begin working toward getting sponsored content deals. The following guidelines will help you understand how to land your deals, selecting which deals to go through with, and how the deal itself actually works.

## When to Start Looking for Sponsorships

The best time to start looking for sponsorships is when you begin reaching a consistent following of a few thousand people. Ultimately, it depends on the specific company that you are looking to get sponsorship with. However, the more followers and unique page visitors you have per month, the better. This is another reason why monitoring your analytics is valuable: it helps you know when to start looking for sponsorships, and it helps you know exactly what you are pitching when you pitch sponsor opportunities to companies.

Ideally, you want to have a minimum of 5,000 followers and unique page viewers on your website before you begin looking for sponsorship deals with smaller, startup companies. When you reach 10,000 and higher you can begin looking for mature companies that are still fairly small in size. These would be mature, independent companies, for example, that have an established following but that are not mass corporations. If you want to start producing sponsored content for massive corporations, you will need upward of 100,000 followers.

So, essentially, the more followers and unique page views you get per month, the larger your deals will become. The larger your deals are, the more money you will get paid per post.

## Landing Sponsorship Deals

Getting sponsorship deals happens in two ways. Early on, it generally starts with you reaching out to companies. Later, you will likely find that companies start reaching out to you. Let's talk about early on, first.

Landing your sponsorship deals will start with you taking your analytics and approaching smaller companies. You want to approach small companies that reflect the unique industry you are writing for, and that sell products or services that your visitors would be most interested in. Then, you want to ask them if they would be interested in having a sponsored post on your website. Often, they will want to know more about you and your analytics before they consider agreeing. However, as long as your analytics support their cause, most smaller companies will be happy to do a sponsored post.

You should note that these posts will be worth a smaller amount. You may only make a couple of hundred dollars or less per post in the beginning. This is okay. The idea is that you are getting started and that you are getting used to these sponsorship deals.

As you begin growing in size and popularity, you can begin approaching more mature companies. Often, these companies will have professional channels of communication. You should always be sure to honor these channels, as this is how proper professionalism on your behalf. Since you are a business approaching another business, you need to ensure that you are viewed from a professional point of view. If you are unsure about who to ask, where, or how, you can always contact them and ask for directions on this information. In many cases, they are happy to provide you with information back.

Always make sure that you approach companies with professionalism. Do not pitch to them like you are trying to get something from them. Instead, pitch to them with authority, asserting what you have to offer to them so that they know that you realize how important the sponsorship is for them, as well as you. Early on, you want to show that you have an intention to create an equal give-and-take partnership that will benefit your mutual audience, rather than coming off as though you are simply trying to earn an extra quick buck.

## How to Ensure the Deal Is Good

Once you start landing sponsorship deals, you need to be sure that you know how to look over the deals. Not every deal is a good one, and therefore you should not automatically assume that it is proper to say yes to any and every deal that comes your way. Instead, you need to make sure that you are looking them over and that they actually are a good deal.

Here is what you need to look for when you are ensuring a deal with a sponsor is good:

- Your Expectations. If you have expectations going into the sponsorship, for example getting free stuff to test for your audience, or being paid, you need to be clear on this from the beginning.

The company you are entering a sponsorship with should be willing to agree to these terms, assuming they are reasonable based on what you are offering them in return.

- Their Expectations. This is where you have to be extra cautious. When you sign a sponsorship agreement with some sponsors, there is a clause that states that you must give the item a positive review whether you like it or not. You should never take these deals. On the off chance that you dislike the product, you will be obligated to lie to your audience. If you get caught lying, your audience will lose trust in you, and therefore you will lose loyalty. This will have a highly negative impact on your bottom line. You should also consider how many times they want you to post, and what you can or cannot say about the company itself. Some companies are fairly free and open with this, but others can get very specific and controlling. Be sure that you are completely aware of what you are getting into before you agree to any terms.

- Payment Method. Assuming you are getting paid for your sponsorship, you should know exactly how the payment is going to work. You should know when it will be released, what conditions need to be met for it to be released, and how you will receive it. If you do not know this, or the terms seem inappropriate or somewhat shady to you, avoid the deal.

It is important that you are always careful on your sponsorship deals in regards to the fine print. Never agree to anything before you know exactly what it is that you are agreeing to. Remember, as a blogger, your readers' loyalty is what results in you getting paid. If you break that loyalty, you will ultimately reduce the amount of income you make. You need to put your readers first, which means always being honest and only backing up products and services that you genuinely believe in.

Sponsorships with Affiliate Deals

Affiliate deals are another form of income entirely, but they often link with sponsorship deals. We are going to discuss both right now so that you understand how these work.

When you get sponsored, many companies will offer you an affiliate link. This typically comes with an exclusive code or coupon that your audience can use to receive a discount with the company that has sponsored your post. This means that you get paid for the post, as well as anytime someone purchases products or services with your code. This results in you getting double-paid. These deals can result in you earning an incredible additional source of income, so always be on the lookout for these opportunities. If you have more say in your deal, you can always suggest or request this to be a part of it, too.

Affiliate deals do not have to be tied to sponsors. Many other companies, such as Amazon, have affiliate programs that you can become a part of. These give you access to unique links, codes, and other tools that you are given to drive your audience to their pages. When your audience lands on their page and shops for something, you are then paid a commission for that. This can be a great way to maximize your income, so it is definitely worth looking out for!

## Sponsorship Agencies

Like advertisement agencies, sponsorship agencies are like a one-stop shop for getting sponsorships. While this typically won't land you with major companies, it is a great way to get started with sponsorships. There are many agencies out there, and they are continually changing. For that reason, there are none that I can currently recommend that will continue to be valid for a long period of time. In general, however, they are fairly easy to find through a quick internet search. Once you have found one, make sure you look up reviews to confirm that it is legitimate. Then, you can go ahead and create an account. The agency will then walk you through getting set up with companies so that they can begin sponsoring your posts! This is a great way to get started and can help you in the outreach process to bring income in.

## How You Get Paid

Getting paid through sponsorships varies. Most often, they will pay you through PayPal, as this is the easiest payment strategy that is globally accepted. You generally get paid prior to posting the agreed upon post. However, if you go through a sponsorship agency, the company may pay the funds to the agency. This means that they will be held in escrow until the company agrees that you have met the terms of your agreement. Then, the funds will be released to you, and you can withdraw them in whatever way is supported by the agency themselves.

# CHAPTER 8

❧

# Monetized Through Products

The final most popular and high paying way that you can monetize your blog is through creating some form of products or services for your clients. The popular products and services are typically an evergreen course, a PDF, an eBook, and other things that can be placed on the site. These are typically based specifically on your expertise and are designed to add "more value" than your blog itself. That way, if people like what they read, they can purchase more and learn more. As a result, you get paid.

## When You Can Start Selling Your Own Products

Technically, you can start creating and selling your own products right away. However, you will likely notice that you don't make a significant return right away. Until your audience begins to grow, you may not make too many sales in the beginning. That is okay, however. Remain dedicated and continue creating. The more you get to know your audience, the more you can tailor your products to serve their needs.

Some blogs begin selling basic content, such as eBooks or pre-recorded specialized webinars right away. As a result, they can make a fairly decent income really close to the time they launch their blog. If you want to do your best to start monetizing instantly, you can begin creating and selling smaller products such as this. This will help you make more money sooner, as well as gain further analytics on your audience and what they are interested in.

## Creating Your Own Products

Creating products to sell on your blog is easy. First, you have to consider your area of expertise and your industry. Then, you have to consider what your audience is most likely to buy. Once you have, you can start creating anything that you think your audience would consume.

If you are unsure, go back and revisit the other high performing blogs in your niche. Look to see what they are selling, and use that as inspiration to help you. Essentially, you want to take an already-popular form of product and customize it to suit your audience, filled with your unique information and expertise.

The majority of products that you would sell through your blog take very minimal investment and can result in you earning a high amount of profit. Typically, you simply have to put together your best information and package it in a way that is easy for your readers to purchase.

In addition to books, services, and courses, you can also sell actual products. Many blogs have made branded products such as cups, t-shirts, hoodies, hats, and other products that they sell on their blog. If they have a particularly popular catch phrase or motto, they will put these onto the products and sell them. Alternatively, they may sell products that are relevant to their niche. For example, if you wrote a crafting and DIY blog, you may create a page on your website where you sell your own creations to your readers.

## Types of Products to Consider

There are many different types of products to consider when you are running a blog. The majority of the products that blogs sell are digital, however some, as we mentioned, are physical. If you are going to offer physical products, you will have to consider your unique niche and how that would work. Since there are so many things to consider for this, we are not going to go deep into detail on what types of physical products you might consider selling. Instead, we are going to focus on digital products. Below is a list of many different digital products and services that you may consider selling on your blog to maximize your income:

- eBooks
- Coaching or mentor services
- Evergreen courses
- Live courses
- Evergreen webinars
- Live webinars
- PDF workbooks
- Templates
- Audio downloads
- Photographs
- Videos
- Graphic design or web elements
- Customized guides (i.e., training diary, food guide, dream journal)
- Checklists
- Software
- Blueprints or plans
- Recipes

These different products are all things that you can create and sell on your blog. Which ones you choose to work with will depend on your niche and how you can customize them to fit your audience.

## How to Sell These Products

Selling the products on your blog is actually simple. First, you want to make a page for your product(s) on your blog. Then, you want to make a post that directs people to this product or service. Refrain from making the post too salesy. Instead, make it informative. Next, you want to talk about it on your social media platforms. Do not make it the highlight of what you talk about, but rather infuse it anywhere that it fits organically. As well, you can share it intentionally a few times per week. You can also pay for ad space to sell your products.

You do not want to bombard your audience with your sales. Otherwise, they are going to feel like you are not a blog but rather a salesperson. Instead, you want to talk about your products or services about 20% of the time and provide other content around 80% of the time. This will ensure that you are easily managing the balance and that you are not overwhelming your audience with salesy posts. Remember, they came to you because you provide value. You cannot change that now and begin only providing value if they pay you. Continue being true to the blog you have always been, but add this additional element for those who want to receive more of what you offer. If you are genuine and loyal to your followers, the majority of them will be genuine and loyal back. This can result in massive profits over time. In fact, many bloggers make several six figures through their products and services that they offer alongside their blog.

**How You Get Paid**

Receiving payment from your blog through your products or services will typically depend on what platform you are using. Generally speaking, you will get paid anytime someone purchases your product or service. How that payment is issued to you, however, will depend. If your platform is connected to a specific platform, like PayPal, your payments will all automatically come in through PayPal. However, if it is not, the platform itself may "hold" your funds until you choose to withdraw them into your bank account, or elsewhere.

You can learn more about how you will get paid by reading the policies and guidelines on your platform, or on the platform, you use to host your sales. Some people prefer to host sales through Etsy or Shopify while hosting their blogs on something like WordPress or Squarespace. If you choose to do this, you will need to read the guidelines for receiving payments through your e-commerce host to make sure that you are clear on how to receive these payments.

# CONCLUSION

∽

Thank you for reading "Make Money Blogging: A Proven Method for 6 Figures A Year."

This book was designed to help you develop a greater understanding of how blogging can be a serious business that can help you earn serious income. If you want to generate six-figure years through blogging, this book can help you do that. Remember, the process of generating a profitable blog is not an art, it's a science. There are specific strategies that can be enforced and things that you must consider to generate the income you desire. Should you follow these steps, however, then it should be easy and feasible for you to generate six figures or more every single year from your blog.

I hope that this book was able to clearly define the steps required for you to host a profitable blog. Instead of blogging being a hobby or an element of your business, blogging can be your business. Blogging is a great way to take your business with you so that you can live and work remotely and do the things that you love to do. Whether you want to travel with your family, enjoy the solitude of the countryside, or simply invest more time in your day-to-day life without the constraints of a 9-to-5 job, blogging is a great way to go.

The next step is to read this book once again and begin enforcing the various steps, in order, to start creating your income! Know that in the beginning, it may feel slow, but if you stay fixated on your vision, it will all come to life. Put your steps together in order, take your time, and focus on creating quality and value. Monitor your analytics and use these as a guide to help move you forward and keep you generating income from your blog. As long as you remain focused and stay on the path of building your blog with these steps, you will be earning six figures in no time.

Blogging is something that does take some time, especially considering the amount of outreach you have to do early on to actually get in contact with your audience. For that reason, I suggest that you get clear on why you are doing this right now. Staying focused, staying committed, and remembering the bigger picture will be heavily necessary for driving you forward toward success. The more effort and value you put in now, however, the more income you stand to make later on. It is those who remain consistent and devoted that make the greatest income through blogging in the end.

Lastly, if you felt this book added value, helped you monetize your blog and maximize your income, and was enjoyable, please take the time to review it on Amazon Kindle. Your honest feedback would be greatly appreciated.

Thank you!